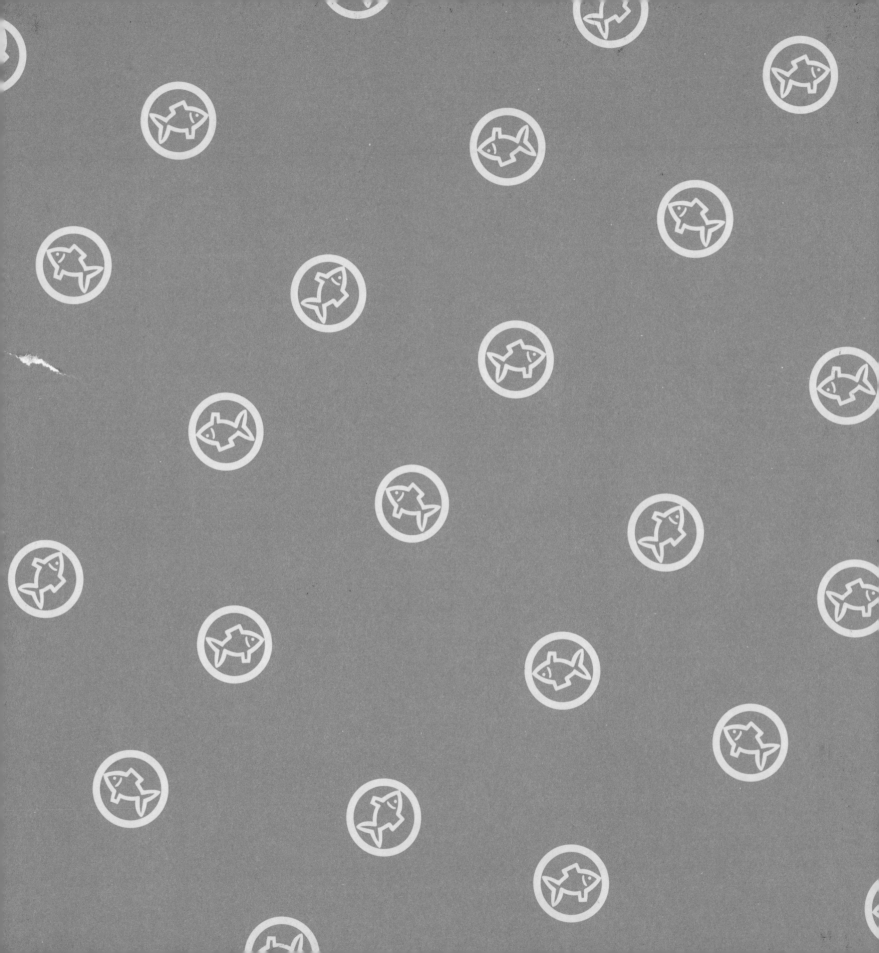

I Am a Sea Turtle

The Life of a Green Sea Turtle

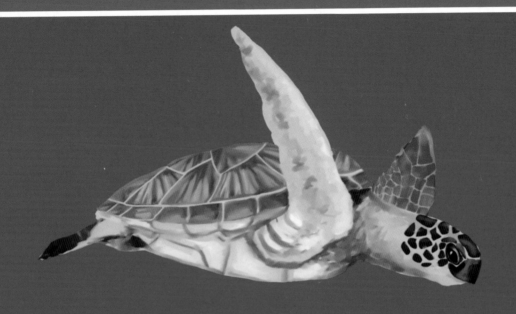

by Darlene R. Stille illustrated by Todd Ouren

Special thanks to our advisers for their expertise:

Susan H. Shane, Ph.D., Biology
University of California at Santa Cruz

Susan Kesselring, M.A., Literacy Educator
Rosemount-Apple Valley-Eagan (Minnesota) School District

I Live in the Ocean

Managing Editors: Bob Temple, Catherine Neitge
Creative Director: Terri Foley
Editors: Nadia Higgins, Patricia Stockland
Editorial Adviser: Andrea Cascardi
Designer: Todd Ouren
Page production: Picture Window Books
The illustrations in this book were prepared digitally.

Picture Window Books
5115 Excelsior Boulevard
Suite 232
Minneapolis, MN 55416
877-845-8392
www.picturewindowbooks.com

Printed in the United States of America.

Library of Congress Cataloging-in-Publication Data
Stille, Darlene R.
I am a sea turtle : the life of a green sea turtle /
by Darlene R. Stille ; illustrated by Todd Ouren.
p. cm. — (I live in the ocean)
Includes bibliographical references (p.   ).
ISBN 1-4048-0597-4 (reinforced lib. bdg.)
1. Green turtle—Juvenile literature. I. Ouren, Todd, ill. II. Title.

QL666.C536S75 2004
597.92'8—dc22   2004000888

I glide silently through the ocean. I look like a flying saucer. I am a sea turtle.

I am called a green sea turtle, but I am more than green. My beautiful shell has swirls of gray, brown, and orange.

Green sea turtles get their name from their color.

Flap, flap, flap. I swim by flapping my front flippers up and down. Under water, I move like a bird in flight.

Reptiles are cold-blooded.
Their bodies don't make their
own heat. A sea turtle's body
is as cold or as warm as the
water around it.

I live with fish. I move like a bird, but I am a reptile.
I stay in warm waters. I swim to the surface
to grab a breath of air.

6

Like most reptiles, I hatched from an egg. The egg I was in was buried in sand. For days, I dug and dug, up, up, up onto the beach.

Sea turtle eggs look like pingpong balls, but they are soft and leathery. This keeps them from cracking when their mother drops them into the underground nest.

Moonlight made the ocean sparkle. With my brothers and sisters, I scrambled toward the water. *Whee!* I dove into a wave.

Most of my brothers and sisters got snatched up by hungry predators near the shore. Not me! I swam like crazy. The deeper I got, the safer I was.

Very few sea turtles make it to adulthood. That's why a mother sea turtle has to lay so many eggs. She may lay as many as 500 eggs in one season.

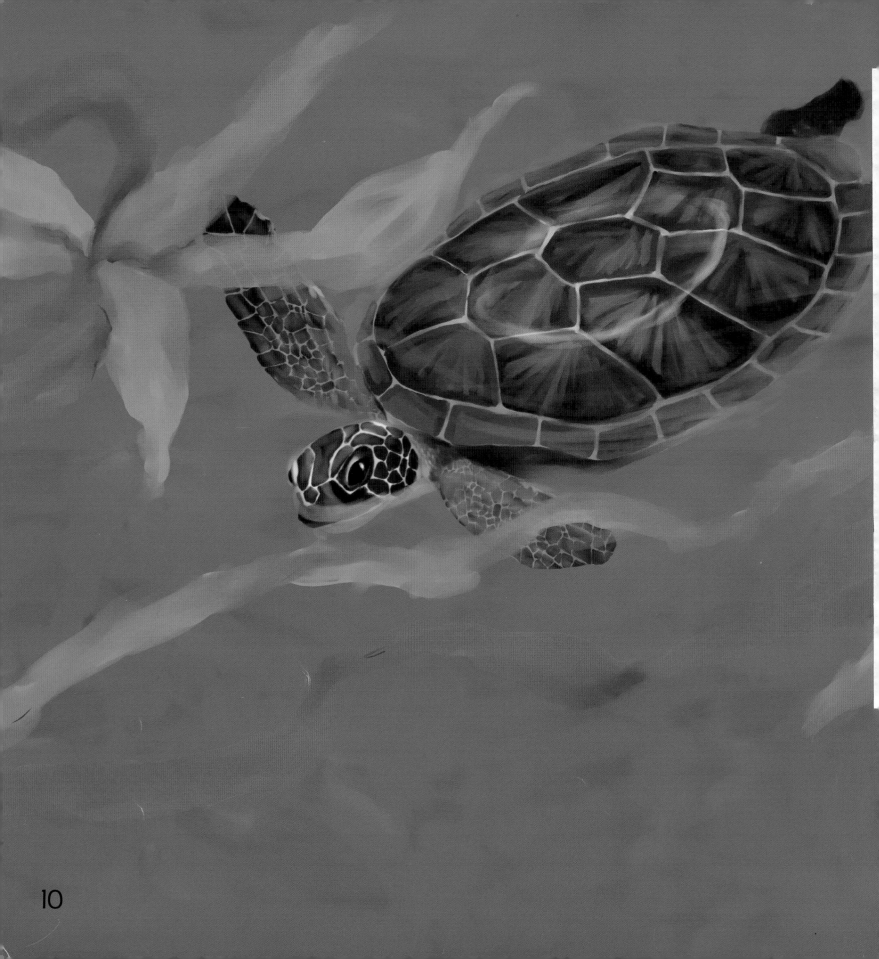

For a while, I drifted on the surface of the water. I hid in patches of floating seaweed and ate small sea animals.

Now I am a grown-up. I mostly eat sea grass and other plants. I swim through the open ocean.

Last year, I swam back to the beach where I was hatched. I swam hundreds and hundreds of miles—and I didn't even need a map.

I didn't stay long. I laid my eggs and hurried back to the water. I left my babies to hatch by themselves.

Every two to four years, green sea turtles swim about 1,300 miles (2,080 kilometers) to return to the exact same beach where they were born. Scientists aren't sure how the turtles can swim so far without getting lost.

We sea turtles are pretty independent. I mostly eat and swim by myself, even if there are other sea turtles around.

In deep water, sea turtles stretch out on the surface of the ocean water and sleep.

Sometimes when I am near shore, I lie by myself under a rocky ledge and take a nap. I can stay under water like this for more than two hours!

16

Every now and then, I like to go to a cleaning station. That's a place where little fish gather.

I stretch my neck while the fish nibble at my shell. They eat the little plants growing there. They get me all cleaned up. *Aaaaahhhhh.*

Sea turtles can't pull their flippers or heads into their shells the way other turtles can.

Life for me isn't always such a breeze. Noise, trash, and bright lights are making my beach yucky.

Pollution is making many of my friends sick. Fishing nets and boat propellers are turning my home into a dangerous place.

Sea turtles are endangered animals. That means all of them might die out. In some countries, it is illegal to harm a sea turtle or its eggs.

19

A lot of people are worried about me. Scientists and lawmakers are looking for ways to keep me safe.

I'm pretty lucky I made it this far. I am 50 years old now. With some help, I could live to be 100!

Sea turtles are among the oldest kinds of animals on Earth. Sea turtles were around during the age of dinosaurs. By keeping beaches and oceans clean, we can keep sea turtles around for many years to come.

Look Closely at a Sea Turtle

Dark top of shell makes the turtle blend in with the dark sea below. This makes it harder for predators to see the turtle from above.

Hard, flexible plates on the shell are called scutes. Scientists can tell the kind of turtle by the number and pattern of scutes.

Shell is sensitive to touch.

Eyes actually see more clearly under water than on land.

Back flippers help the sea turtle steer as it swims.

Light bottom of shell makes the turtle blend in with the light sky above. This makes it harder for hungry creatures to see the turtle from below.

Front flippers are long and wide for paddling through the water.

Sea turtles don't have teeth. Sawlike ridges on the jaws are good for cutting through tough seaweed.

Fun Facts

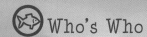 Who's Who

There are seven species (or kinds) of sea turtles: the green sea turtle, the flatback, the hawksbill, the loggerhead, the Kemp's ridley, the olive ridley, and the leatherback. Sea turtles are found in warm oceans throughout the world.

The Biggest Ones

Sea turtles are the biggest kind of turtle. The largest sea turtle is the leatherback. Its shell can be 8 feet (2 1/2 meters) long. A leatherback can weigh more than 1,500 pounds (675 kilograms).

Turn Off the Lights!

Some scientists think baby sea turtles find the sea by following the light of the moon sparkling on the water. Bright lights near a beach can confuse the turtles, though. Sometimes, baby turtles head away from the ocean toward parking lots, shopping malls, or roads and highways.

 ## Sea Senses

Sea turtles have good senses. They can hear very low sounds. They also have a strong sense of smell.

 ## There, There

When a sea turtle climbs on land, it looks as if she is crying. Those tears don't mean the turtle is sad. The tears are how the turtle's body gets rid of extra salt that it has taken in from salty seawater. The tears actually help the turtle by washing sand out of her eyes as she digs her nest.

 ## Temperature Matters

The temperature of the nest determines whether an egg will produce a male turtle or a female turtle. Cooler temperatures produce more males. Warmer temperatures produce more females.

Glossary

cold-blooded—an animal that cannot make its own heat; it is as cold or as warm as the air or water around it

endangered—when an animal is one of the few of its kind left in the world; people worry that endangered animals might all die

hatch—to break out of an egg

pollution—dirty, smelly waste that makes air and water dangerous to living things

predator—an animal that hunts other animals for food

reptile—a cold-blooded animal with lungs and scaly skin

To Learn More

At the Library

Arnosky, Jim. *Turtle in the Sea.* New York: G. P. Putnam's Sons, 2002.

Bair, Diane, and Pamela Wright. *Sea Turtle Watching.* Mankato, Minn.: Capstone Press, 2000.

Dunbier, Sally. *Sea Turtles.* Hauppage, N.Y.: Barron's, 2000.

Pirotta, Saviour. *Turtle Bay.* New York: Farrar, Straus and Giroux, 1997.

On the Web

FactHound offers a safe, fun way to find Web sites related to this book. All of the sites on FactHound have been researched by our staff. *www.facthound.com*

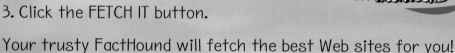

1. Visit the FactHound home page.
2. Enter a search word related to this book, or type in this special code: 0404805974
3. Click the FETCH IT button.

Your trusty FactHound will fetch the best Web sites for you!

Index

Look for all the books in this series:

I Am a Dolphin
The Life of a Bottlenose Dolphin

I Am a Fish
The Life of a Clown Fish

I Am a Sea Turtle
The Life of a Green Sea Turtle

I Am a Seal
The Life of an Elephant Seal

I Am a Shark
The Life of a Hammerhead Shark

I Am a Whale
The Life of a Humpback Whale